Echoes Of Seasons.

Jui Purohit

BookLeaf Publishing

India | USA | UK

Dedication

Dedicated to my family and friends who have always supported me in my writing journey, through all the seasons!

Preface

This collection of poems seeks to capture the essence of ebb and flow of seasons. Along with a kaleidoscope of colours, seasons bring in happiness, transformation and a symphony of emotions in our lives. So readers, poetry lovers, indulge in this special treat of 'Echoes of Seasons'.

Acknowledgements

A big thank you to all the people in my life who have inspired me, encouraged me and appreciated my passion to write. You are the reason I was motivated to keep writing and follow my fervour.

1. Still frozen!

I'm still here frozen in time
where you left me....
Should I continue to believe or open my eyes to see?
It is a dream or is it a hazy puzzle?
If I hug you will you too crumble?
We will meet at the end of the horizon
With this deceit, heart pacifies me from dusk to dawn.....
Glitters and corals, sun rises and sets as per the drill
But my life has lost all the seasons and the thrill!

2. Come to me.....

Come to me when the winters are bleak
I will keep you cosy and warm,
As the frost melts, I'll shield you against cold
Protecting you from any harm....
Come to me when summers are scorching
To cool down under my wings,
Wiping off that sweat and toil
To relax, oblivious of onerous things....
Come to me when its pouring merciless
I will keep you safe
Wrapped around in umbrella of my arms
Repartee bout future and reminiscing yesterdays.....

3. Winter forever....

Loneliness pent up inside her
Seasons just changed
But spring in her life had turned into winter forever!

4. Goodbye!

Regrets will wash away moments we spent together,
So, if we meet on a balmy summer day, some day or other,
Let's just part ways with a smile,
Before the goodbye, lets walk side by side for a mile.

5. Ruins of time....

5

Ruins of time
Deserts of garden
Separated by destiny
Lost forgotten?
Seasons have changed
But have hearts altered?
Silencing the sprouts of affection
Sufferings of souls tortured!

6. Moonbeams.

Blue light from moonbeams
Did you follow me secretly?
As I walked passed the cold winters
To grab the spring illicitly
Worn out from the freezing breezes
And the endless nights chilly
Pursuit of a tepid shelter
Through the ebb and flow hilly
Did you want to unmask my spirit?
Spotlight on the troubled soul in the alley!

7. I will fly to you....

If you tell me your longing
I will fly to you like wind
Stars like diamonds, shining
I will place them in your ring
Soft whispers of night
And yearning of thousand years
Winter's cold delight
Calm, with me, under the warm layers!

8. Loving me is not an obligation.

Loving me is not an obligation,
Reciprocating is not compulsion,
With no expectations whatsoever
Let me fill my heart with ardourous emotions.....

Love cannot be undone now,
Seasons ought to change and how,
Unrequited affection of my heart
Will remain frigid like winters, somewhow....

9. Spring of my life!

You are my heart, you are my home
Spring of my life after the winters are done.....
Monsoon drizzles, cool and refreshing
Warmth and fondness, august and impressing!

10. Sping is here....

Spring is here with blossoms around
My soul's filled with fragrance earthbound
Eyes sparkle with yellows and pinks
Storing all the hues without blinks.

11. Kaleidoscope of seasons!

Brushstrokes of spring's vibrant hue
Blossoms and sprouts, all anew,
Petals adorning the soils rustic
Bees on flowers brisk and quick,
Kaleidoscope of season enchants
Colourful canvas of flora and plants!

12. Like a butterfly.

Like a butterfly....
Hues on my wings
Blossoms around
Search of nectar
Crest to ground!

Lush verdant
Flowers whispering
Balmy sun
Welcoming spring!

Flapping quietly
Those tiny wings
Merrily gliding
Through amber tints!

13. Spring that we are waiting for.....

Why did you hug me dearly in my dreams?
It hurts when I wake up
You look at me like a warm sunshine
And it all vanishes into a slump.....

Dreams look far fetched now
Everything is just melting away
What's real and what is illusion
My heart and soul cannot say.....

Spring that we were waiting for
Would it ever arrive?
World where we would coexist has crashed
How do we survive?

14. Mayflower!

Mayflower, you are to me.....
Lily that blooms only in May,
Otherwise you may not see it sway,
Willy nilly I try to cling and call,
Getting worked up and my work to stall,
Yet, there's no trace of you,
Fathomless, to which island you flew,
Just the emptiness surrounding my vision,
Counting my breaths in search of a reason,
Will I see you bloom again my Mayflower?
Ceasing the fragrance in my heart forever!

15. Sweltering Summers.

Sweltering summers
Warming my loneliness
Longer days and my languid dress!

Why don't the worries fade
In this unwished heat
Emptiness brings no delight!

16. Golden summers!

Warming the air summer arrives
Laughter echoes and nonchalantly thrives,
Shimmery golds across the canvas spreads
Eternal azure and dreams endless!

17. First drop of rain.

First drop of rain falls
Petrichor lingers through night
Primal treat of monsoons
Drenched leaves, picturesque sight!

18. Monsoon's symphony!

Rhythmic drops as if monsoon's symphony
Soothing melody, hushing the cacophony,
Renewal, growth and germination around
Verdure splendid across drenched ground!

19. Serene rains.

19

Thunderous sounds scary at times,
Sky grows dark and the wind chimes,
Brimming with aqua, the clouds assemble,
Rains pour down and the hay trembles,
Streams pervasive merge and convene,
Withered essences now reviving serene!

20. Him and the ardent rains!

Is he the one? And your heart beats rapidly,
As if affirming, doubt into conviction, aptly,
Deep orange and yellow skies, beautiful,
Hues amorous entwined in the ambience, colourful,
Souls drenched in ardent rains, slake,
Sunsets like these brim your eyes, awake!

21. Haiku.

Symphony of seasons
Golden hues and rains
Quenching parched earth....

22. Culmination!

Culmination, nature's scenic dance,
Before the deep slumber, it's the final chance
Shadows deep and the fading lights,
Coral glows and autumny nights!

23. Scarlet leaves....

Scarlet leaves and maple dust
Autumn's farewell and summer's trust
Crimson turns to silver bright
Gentle winds and longer nights....

Earth lies dormant, ambience still
Unruly mornings turning chill
Barren trees like skeletal frames
Frozen lakes, abandoned lanes....

24. Silence of mountains.

Echoes of my heartbeats loud and clear,
Dew on wildflowers like an unwelcomed tear
Secrets of wind, it whispers through trees tall,
Seasons just change, spring after fall,
Shifts happen, but the mystical silence of mountains
remains.....

Are you here for inner peace?
All that's broken, can you mend piece by piece?
Will you find your soul in this stillness?
Through this clamour, will you ascertain calmness?
Questions haunt me, but the mystical silence of
mountains remains.....

25. Horizons of seasons.

Feels like you are on the other side of earth,
Yet the seasons will merge at some point
Metamorphosis of misery in mirth!

26. The fall.

And when the fall arrives
Yellow leaves bid goodbyes
Gliding down to the ground,
Retiring from the trees
Forthwith, as if at ease!

27. Seasons change.

Forget the past,
As seasons change at last,
Don't keep dwelling on unhappy moments
Making miserable your present!

28. Hold me in your eyes!

Hold me in your eyes
Through the foliage of autumn
Springs are soon to arrive
Making the frigid less gruesome.....
Wait for me to hug you
Floral whiff and corals dance
Azure skies and morning dew
Drowning all the worries at once!

29. Known yet unknown!

Echoes of my heartbeats loud and clear,
Dew on wildflowers like an unwelcomed tear
Secrets of wind, it whispers through trees tall,
Seasons just change, spring after fall,
Shifts happen, but the mystical silence of mountains
remains.....

Are you here for inner peace?
All that's broken, can you mend piece by piece?
Will you find your soul in this stillness?
Through this clamour, will you ascertain calmness?
Questions haunt me, but the mystical silence of
mountains remains.....

30. Let me swing.....just one more time.

Let me swing just one more time,
On the boat of happiness climb,
Let me be a little girl once more,
Enjoying little things to the core.....

Let me swing and rise up high,
Bidding melancholy a goodbye,
Going back to the seasons I yearn,
Pristine lessons to learn, unlearn.....

How carefree was I then!
Burdens were lighter and bruises didn't pain,
Now life's full of uncertainty,
To swing happily is a novelty!

www.ingramcontent.com/pod-product-compliance
Lightning Source LLC
La Vergne TN
LVHW010834200726
843508LV00012B/2600